FOOD

Christopher McHugh

Wayland

Discovering Art

Cover: Le Déjeuner *painted by the French Impressionist artist Claude Monet.*

Editor: Rosemary Ashley
Designer: David Armitage
Special Consultant: Pauline Ridley, Lecturer in
History of Art and Design at the University of
Brighton and the Open University.

This edition published in 1994
by Wayland (Publishers) Ltd

First published in 1992 by
Wayland (Publishers) Ltd
61 Western Road, Hove
East Sussex BN3 1JD

British Library Cataloguing in Publication Data
McHugh, Christopher
   Food. – (Discovering Art Series)
   I. Title.   II. Series
   704.9496413

HARDBACK ISBN 0-7502-0509-1
PAPERBACK ISBN 0-7502-1338-8

Typeset by Type Study, Scarborough, England
Printed and bound in Italy by G. Canale & C.S.p.A., Turin

Contents

1 Food in art

Food is so important to us that it is not surprising it has been shown many times in art all over the world and throughout history. In this book we take a look at some of the many ways that people have shown food in their art; from food goddesses to feasts, and from picnics to tinned soup.

On these pages we see two pictures of food painted by Italian artists who lived at about the same time – in the 1500s. But the two pictures show very different subjects and are painted in very different styles.

Picture **1** on this page is a painting by Caravaggio called *Supper at Emmaus*. It is a religious scene, showing Jesus

1 Supper at Emmaus *by Caravaggio. Reproduced by courtesy of the Trustees, the National Gallery, London.*

2 Winter *by Giuseppe
Arcimboldo. If you look
closely you can see that the
vegetables and fruits form the
top half of a man, with a
wintry scene in the
background.*

Christ sharing a meal with his followers. He has come back
from the dead after being put to death on the cross. Look
how dark Caravaggio has made the shadows in his picture,
and how clearly he shows the differences between the
shadows and the lighter areas. See how he has made
St Peter's hand appear to come out towards us as we look
at the picture. These clever tricks make Caravaggio's
painting look very real. Although he died when quite
young he was a very famous artist during his lifetime.

Picture **2** is a strange painting by Giuseppe Arcimboldo,
who was also a well-known artist during his lifetime. His
picture shows a pile of vegetables and fruit on a table in
front of a window. If you look at the picture for a while you
will see that the vegetables seem to become a person. Or
perhaps you saw the person first before you realized it was
really a pile of food!

2 Food in the ancient world

Pictures **3** and **4** are scenes from ordinary life in Ancient Egypt, which hardly changed over thousands of years. This unchanging lifestyle was partly due to plentiful food which the River Nile and careful farming helped to provide. The land occupied by the Ancient Egyptians was the valley of the Nile. Large areas of the land flooded every year and this made the soil very fertile. The Egyptians grew large quantities of wheat in the Nile Valley.

3 An Ancient Egyptian painting showing a farmer ploughing a field. The plough is pulled by an ox. British Museum, London.

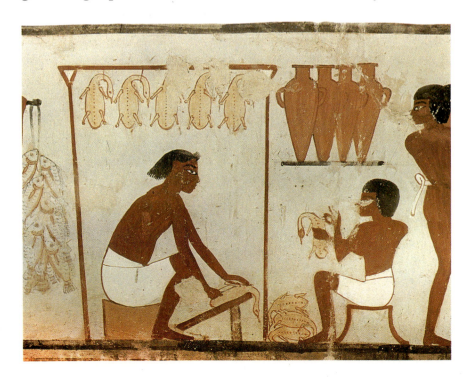

4 Another painting from Ancient Egypt; this shows a kitchen scene. It was painted on the wall of a tomb.

Picture **3** shows a field being ploughed ready for the planting of seed gathered from the previous year's wheat crop. The picture is painted on papyrus, a kind of paper made from a plant which grew along the river banks. The Egyptians ate other foods too, as we can see in picture **4**. This is a wall-painting showing kitchen workers plucking feathers from birds and preparing them for cooking. These are probably geese caught on hunting trips in the marshes along the banks of the Nile. Can you see the fish hanging up against the kitchen wall to the left of the picture, and earthenware pots, probably holding oil or wine, stacked on the shelves?

Two of the earliest and greatest civilizations in Europe were those of the Greeks and Romans. Picture **5** is part of a picture painted on a large pot as a decoration by an Ancient Greek artist. It shows the Greek goddesses, Demeter and Persephone, sending the gift of wheat to Earth with a messenger. Actually, the wheat was almost certainly brought to Greece from Egypt, but the Greeks preferred to think of it as a gift from the gods.

5 *The goddesses in this painting on an Ancient Greek vase are Demeter and her daughter Persephone. Demeter was the Greek goddess of agriculture and she could give or prevent good harvests. British Museum, London.*

Pictures **6** and **7** are Roman and both show people at banquets. Picture **6** is a painting on a wall, showing a rather easy-going feast with people chatting as servants bring in the food. Picture **7** is a relief, which is a picture carved into the surface of a wall so that some areas stick out from the background. The relief is clearly part of a wall – you can see the sloping top edges of the picture which are the edges of the wall itself. This is why the arrangement is much tidier and stiffer than the wall-painting (picture **6**), although the people still seem to be chatting and enjoying their meal. You can see other pictures of banquets and meals in the next chapter.

6 (above) A banqueting scene painted on a wall in Pompeii, during the days of the Roman Empire.

3 Feasts

7 (left) A relief sculpture showing people enjoying a meal in Ancient Rome.

8 (above) Peasant Wedding by Pieter Brueghel the Elder. In this picture the artist has shown people enjoying lots of food and drink at a wedding. Kunsthistorisches Museum, Vienna.

The big meal, or feast, has always played an important part in people's lives, marking special occasions and involving lots of people. Think of a time when you have been invited to a special meal, or seen one on television or read about one in a book. There is often a feast at weddings so that families and friends can celebrate the new marriage. Often people have feasts at festivals, like Christmas or Id al-Fitr or on their birthdays. Pictures **8** and **9** show two very different kinds of feast. One is an indoor feast for ordinary people who are celebrating a wedding; the other is an outdoor feast for rich people and shows the easy life that they enjoyed.

9 La Chasse by Charles van Loo. The painting shows rich people picnicking in the countryside while a deer hunt is going on. Roy Miles Fine Paintings, London.

Picture **8** (overleaf) was painted by the Flemish artist Pieter Brueghel in the 1500s. Picture **9** (above) was painted by the French artist Charles van Loo two hundred years later. The two paintings tell us a lot about the differences in the lives of working people and rich people living in the sixteenth and eighteenth centuries. What kind of food and drink can you see in each picture? How do you think the artists show the differences between the way people lived? For example, look at the plates, bowls and dishes that the foods are eaten from. Can you see any differences in the actual foods the people are eating?

We can also compare picture **9** with the picture on the cover of this book by Claude Monet, painted in the nineteenth century. Both pictures show people having a picnic. Van Loo's picture shows lots of little stories about the people at the picnic, whereas Monet's painting shows a picnic table in a garden with only a child and two ladies nearby. He is more interested in painting the sunlight in the garden than in painting 'stories'.

In picture **10** we are shown a rather different sort of meal. This painting was made by Vincent van Gogh, who lived at the end of the nineteenth century. In it we see a very poor family sharing a simple meal. The picture is called *The Potato Eaters* because this is all the family have for their meal. Can you see anything in this painting which makes it similar to Caravaggio's painting (picture **1** on page 4)? For example, how does van Gogh show the light areas and shadows in his painting?

10 The Potato Eaters *by Vincent van Gogh. In this painting the artist shows very poor people eating a meal consisting only of potatoes and cups of tea. Van Gogh Museum, Amsterdam.*

4 Food around the world

11 *(left) Clay pots in the form of Maize Goddesses. They were made by the Mochica people who lived in South America about 1,500 years ago.*

12 *(opposite) A beautiful Navaho woven blanket which shows the importance of the maize plant to the Amerindians. Private Collection, New York.*

Those of us who live in western countries have the choice of many different kinds of food. We can eat it fresh or dried, tinned or frozen; and it can be prepared in many different ways. But in the past, and still in many parts of the world, just one plant or animal can be the main type of food for a particular group of people. This is called a 'staple' food.

In the Americas, especially before the arrival of Europeans in the 1500s, maize (or corn as it is often called) was a staple food for many people. Maize is often shown in the art of the original peoples of the Americas (called Amerindians). In fact, maize was so important to these peoples that they often believed it was given to them as a special gift from a god, or sometimes that it was a god itself. Picture 11 shows clay pots from a part of South America that is now Peru. They were made by the Mochica people and they show maize goddesses. Can you see how their shapes and bumpy skins make them look like corn cobs?

13 *Two fish painted on tree bark with paints made from different coloured earth. It was made by an Australian Aboriginal artist.*

Picture **12** shows a blanket made by Navaho Amerindians from the deserts of the USA. This was made in about 1880, but it is based on pictures that their ancestors made in the sand in earlier times. It shows the spirits (or gods) of rain and thunder on either side of the maize plant, and the rainbow spirit stretched outside and below all of them. Thunder storms brought the rain needed to make the maize grow in desert regions and the rainbow spirit was thought to have given maize to the people in the first place. If you compare this picture with picture **5** on page 7 you will see that these gods are not so realistic as the Greek goddesses, who seem to be more like real women.

Picture **13** is a painting on tree bark made by an Australian Aboriginal artist. Aborigines often make pictures on bark, or on rocks and other natural objects found in the wild. Their pictures are often of animals, such as the fish shown here, which they need to eat to stay alive, but which they also believe to be special and sacred.

Many parts of Asia have very ancient histories, as old as any in Europe or the Americas. There are many marvellous examples of art from those far off times that still exist. They show us about how people lived in India, China, Japan and other countries of the Asian continent all those years ago.

Picture **14** is a very old Chinese painting, made about ten centuries ago. It was painted on silk and it includes many details – spot the dog lying under the table! Can you see how the artist has drawn the table, tilting it upwards through the picture so he can show more of each person sitting at it? The painting is meant to show elegant life at court, where the meal is an important social event. Notice the bowls on the table and the long serving spoon. The clothes which the people are wearing are clearly not very practical; they are too fussy for ordinary everyday living.

14 (above) Banquet and Concert, *a painting made a thousand years ago in China, showing people dining at the Emperor's palace. Palace Museum, Taipei.*

16 (opposite) *A print showing the Japanese tea ceremony. It was made in Japan in the early twentieth century. Victoria and Albert Museum, London.*

Picture **15** was painted on paper to illustrate a story. It was made in Persia (present-day Iran), and it shows life in a desert camp, including the preparation of food, which was of course an important part of camp life. Can you see all the different jobs that people are doing to prepare the meal?

Picture **16** is a Japanese wood-block print. It shows a tea ceremony, which is a special event in Japan. Tea is made and shared in a very special way. The ceremony is much more important than simply drinking a cup of tea. Although this picture was made many centuries later than picture **14** (opposite), can you see how in some ways the two pictures are alike? In ancient times many ideas, for instance about art and ways of living, were passed on from China to Japan.

15 *A picture showing part of a story in an old manuscript, or book. Teheran Museum.*

5 Meals in the Middle Ages

The Middle Ages is the name given to the period in Europe between the end of the Roman Empire and the Renaissance (from about AD 500 to 1500). The years from about 500 to 1000 are sometimes called the Dark Ages. It was a time of violence and confusion in Europe but gradually Christianity spread across the continent and life became more organized. Here are some pictures from the Middle Ages showing food.

Picture **17** is from a French calendar of about 1200. It illustrates the months of July and August by showing the cutting and gathering of the wheat crop and then the threshing (or beating) of it to separate the grains of wheat from the straw.

Picture **18** is a painting made in England at about the same time. It illustrates a religious story, showing a wedding feast at Cana, where Jesus changed water into

17 *A picture showing harvesting, made in France in the Middle Ages.*

18 The Marriage at Cana, *a painting of a Bible story found in a manuscript which was written by hand. Both pictures on this page were made around AD 1200.*

19 *A picture illustrating a French story called* The Romance of Renaud de Montauban. *It was painted about five hundred years ago.*

wine when all the real wine had been drunk. Notice how Jesus and his parents and the guests are painted larger than the servants in the picture, even though they are further away. Can you see how in pictures **17** and **18** dark outlines have been drawn around the figures? This makes them stand out.

Like the calendar picture (**17**), picture **19** was also made in France, but about two hundred years later. The artist uses his skill and the subject itself to make things appear further away from us, such as the tiles on the floor which are painted smaller as the floor goes further away. Although the artist has used outlines, they are finer than those in pictures **17** and **18**, and they help to give the figures in the picture a sense of movement, rather than to fix them as flat, still shapes.

6 Food on the table

A special kind of painting, showing objects (usually on a table and indoors) is called a 'still life'. Very often, still life pictures show food or objects to do with food. We have already seen a very strange still life in picture **2**, on page 5. Picture **30** on page 27 is also a rather unusual still life, as you will see. The pictures in this chapter show us more straightforward still lifes, painted at very different times in history.

20 *A Roman painting on the wall of a rich person's house in Pompeii, in southern Italy, from around AD 1. The painting was protected because it was covered in volcanic lava from Mount Vesuvius.*

Picture **20** is a very old painting, made on a wall in the Roman town of Pompeii. It comes from a period usually called Graeco-Roman, because the style of painting in this period was invented by the Greeks but made popular throughout their empire by the Romans. It dates from about AD 1. As you can see, it shows a glass and some peaches on shelves. Picture **21**, on the other hand, was made in the middle of the 1600s. It was painted by the Dutch artist Pieter Claesz, and shows several kinds of food on a table covered with a cloth and with a vine in the background.

The basic idea of each picture is similar, showing as realistically as possible the things which help to make up a comfortable life. Considering how old it is, picture **20** is extremely lifelike. But Claesz, like the two painters on the following pages, was able to use oil paint. This allowed

21 Breakfast Still Life with a Crab *by Pieter Claesz. Rafael Valls Gallery, London.*

22 Still Life with Jug and
Fruit *by Paul Cézanne.*
National Gallery of Oslo.

artists to work very carefully, adding layers of colour and building up textures to create an even more realistic picture.

Paul Cézanne and Paul Gauguin were both French artists, working in the second half of the nineteenth century. They each made pictures rather like the Impressionist painters (see pages 24 and 25), but their style of painting became slightly different and they are known as Post-Impressionists, because they came after the Impressionists. Vincent van Gogh who painted *The Potato Eaters*, picture **10** on page 11, is also known as a

Post-Impressionist because of the work he did later on in his life.

Cézanne's painting, **22**, is a still life of fruit and a jug on a table. It seems quite a simple picture, but can you see how the artist shows the light shining on the fruit and on the jug? This painting has much in common with picture **23**, *Still life with Mangoes*, painted by Gauguin. Each picture is a simple arrangement of fruit and other objects on a table. If you look carefully, you can see the marks made by the artist's brush as he painted the picture. Each picture is painted with rich, strong colours and each artist uses dark outlines to make the shapes of the objects stand out a little from the background.

How would you describe the differences between the two pictures, for example in the kind of background shown? One of these artists lived part of his life in a tropical country. Can you tell from these two paintings which artist this was?

23 Still Life with Mangoes
by Paul Gauguin. Christie's, London.

7 Food in northern Europe

During the 1600s a number of well-known artists were working in the northern part of the Netherlands. Among them were Vermeer and Rembrandt, and you can see paintings by these two great artists on these pages.

Jan Vermeer's painting *The Maid with a Milk Jug* (picture **24**) shows a young woman working in a kitchen with everyday objects. Vermeer, one of the world's most famous painters, enjoyed showing the effects of light and the different textures of objects. See how he has made the

24 The Maid with a Milk Jug *by Jan Vermeer. Rijksmuseum, Amsterdam.*

crusts on the loaves look crisp. He painted with oil paint and probably used something called a camera obscura (a kind of early camera) which helped him to see the appearance of light and shadow more clearly.

Rembrandt is another world-famous artist. *The Flayed Ox* (picture **25**) is an unusual picture, but there are earlier pictures like this which perhaps gave Rembrandt the idea of painting a dead animal which has been skinned and hung up. Compared to this picture of food being prepared, the Egyptian kitchen in picture **4** (page 6) seems rather gentle.

Picture **26** is by the English artist William Hogarth, who lived about a hundred years after Rembrandt. His painting also shows part of an animal's carcass, skinned ready for cooking. In Hogarth's picture the meat is not shown in great detail but becomes part of a funny story – can you see how happy the monk is to see the arrival of such a large piece of beef? Rembrandt uses his picture not to tell a story but to show all the texture and detail of the hanging ox-meat.

25 The Flayed Ox *by Rembrandt. Flayed means skinned, and Rembrandt has painted the animal's carcass hanging up ready to be carved into joints of beef. Glasgow City Art Gallery, Scotland.*

26 The Roast Beef of Old England *or* The Calais Gate *by William Hogarth. Hogarth himself can be seen on the left, about to be arrested as a spy for making this drawing of a scene in a French town. Tate Gallery, London.*

8 Food and drink in the modern world

Pictures **27** and **28** on these pages were painted by two Impressionist painters, Edouard Manet and Edgar Degas. The group of Impressionist painters, which included Claude Monet, who painted the picture on the cover of this book, worked in France at the end of the last century. They were called Impressionists because they recorded impressions of light in their work, which they did often on the spot and very quickly.

These pictures show favourite subjects of some of the Impressionists, which were the bars and cafés of Paris. Manet's painting, picture **27**, shows the food and drink on

27 Bar at the Folies Bergère *by Edouard Manet. An acrobat's feet can be seen reflected at the top of the mirror behind the bar. Courtauld Institute, London.*

sale at the bar of a night-club. It describes the enjoyable, exciting side of drinking. Picture **28**, by Degas, shows a very different side of drinking. Absinthe was a very strong, cheap drink which is now forbidden because of its poisonous effects, and the two people in Degas' painting show us just what bad effects drink can have – the couple look very gloomy and unhappy.

28 At the Café, *also known as* Absinthe, *by Edgar Degas. Degas seems to have left out the legs that hold up the table! Musée d'Orsay, Paris.*

The painting of a wheat harvest by Emile Bernard (picture **29**) was made later in the nineteenth century than pictures **27** and **28**. The bright colours, lines and clear shapes are perhaps a little like pictures **17**, **18** and **19** in chapter 5. In fact, Bernard did take ideas about making pictures from the art of the Middle Ages, including stained glass windows in very old French churches.

Picture **30**, *Grandma's Hearth Stone*, by the American artist John Haberle, shows all sorts of objects above and around a fireplace. The painting gives us a cosy, homely feeling, but the artist's real idea is to play games with the way things are shown in the picture. He has painted a frame in his picture around the fireside objects, but then he paints certain objects, such as the walking stick and mantelpiece, as if they are sticking out past the frame. This kind of picture is sometimes called *trompe l'oeil*, or deception of the eye, meaning that the eye is 'tricked' into believing that things on a flat surface actually stick out into real space.

Picture **31** is a painting by the American Pop artist Andy Warhol. It is a screen print showing a can of soup, almost

30 Grandma's Hearth Stone *by John Haberle. The artist has played tricks in his picture, trying to make us believe that some of the painted objects are actually real. Detroit Institute of Arts, USA.*

31 Campbell's Soup, *a screen print made by Andy Warhol. Wolverhampton Art Gallery, England. © 1992 The Andy Warhol Foundation for the Visual Arts/ARS, New York.*

as if it were an advertisement for the soup. Many of Warhol's pictures are like this, made to look as if they should be on a poster rather than framed and hanging in an art gallery. In fact, it is this sense of being something that actually belongs to the ordinary, everyday world which makes this picture interesting. See if you can find a picture in a magazine advertisement which you think should really be in a frame and hanging on the wall in a picture gallery.

Who are the artists and where are their works?

Giuseppe Arcimboldo (c1530–93) Italian
An artist who became very famous during his lifetime for paintings of faces made up of objects such as vegetables, flowers and fruit. His work can be seen in some of the larger collections of paintings in European cities. Picture **2**, page 5.

Emile Bernard (1868–1941) French
Bernard was a friend of Paul Gauguin and the two worked together in Pont Aven, a village in Brittany, France. Later, Bernard was influenced by the ideas of Paul Cézanne. His paintings can be seen at the Musée d'Orsay in Paris, France. Picture **27**, page 27.

Pieter Brueghel (the Elder) (c1525–69) Flemish
Sometimes called 'Peasant Bruegel', Pieter the Elder was the most famous in a family of artists. Two of his sons (Jan and Pieter the Younger) were also successful painters. His works can be seen in major collections in the USA and Europe. Picture **14**, page 9.

Caravaggio (1573–1609) Italian
This artist developed a way of painting using very dark shadows and brightly lit areas in his pictures. He would often take ordinary people from the streets into his studio and would paint them quickly straight on to his canvases in a very realistic way, which was unusual in his time. His pictures can be seen in major collections around the world, including the National Gallery in London. Picture **1**, page 4.

Paul Cézanne (1839–1906) French
Cézanne took some ideas about painting from the Impressionists, especially their ideas about the colour of light. But he wanted to take their ideas further, and to make more solid pictures using their techniques. He is called a Post-Impressionist and has had a huge influence on many famous artists who came after him. His paintings can be seen in many major art collections, especially the Musée d'Orsay in Paris, and the National, Courtauld Institute and Tate Galleries in London. Picture **22**, page 20.

Pieter Claesz (c1596–1661) Dutch
He was one of many Dutch artists who specialized in still life paintings in the seventeenth century. He particularly liked painting food on breakfast tables. His paintings can be seen at the National Gallery in London and in collections in the Netherlands. Picture **21**, page 19.

Edgar Degas (1834–1917) French
He was a member of the Impressionist group of painters although he disliked the name and refused to use it. Degas was one of the first artists to use photography to help him make his paintings. You can see his works in galleries all over the world, especially in the Musée d'Orsay in Paris, and at the Victoria and Albert Museum, the Tate, Courtauld Institute and National Gallery in London. Also in Cambridge, Edinburgh, Glasgow and Liverpool. Picture **27**, page 25.

Paul Gauguin (1848–1903) French
A painter and sculptor who, like Cézanne, took ideas from the Impressionists but wanted to develop them further. He is therefore known as a Post-Impressionist. Some of his most famous pictures are of subjects in the Polynesian islands in the Pacific Ocean, where he spent the last years of his life. His works can be found in collections all over the world, especially the Musée d'Orsay in Paris, in the Tate, National and Courtauld Institute Galleries in London, and in Edinburgh, Glasgow, Manchester and Newcastle. Picture **23**, page 21.

Vincent van Gogh (1853–90) Dutch
Van Gogh was born in the Netherlands but painted many of his best-known pictures in France. He was influenced by the work of Dutch painters of the past, by the bright colours of Japanese prints, and most importantly, by the Impressionist painters. His work can be seen in important collections all over the world, and especially in the Musée d'Orsay in Paris and Van Gogh Museum in Amsterdam; also in the National, Tate and Courtauld Institute Galleries in London. Picture **10**, page 11.

John Haberle (1858–1933) American
Haberle is best known for his slightly odd and rather funny paintings of everyday objects. He played games with the way he showed these objects, trying to surprise the viewer with tricks about what is real and what is in his painting. Most of his work is in the USA and can be seen especially in collections in Philadelphia, the town in which he lived. Picture **30**, page 27.

William Hogarth (1697–1764) British
One of England's most famous painters. He painted portraits and also pictures with scenes from ordinary life. Many of his pictures showed ideas about good and bad behaviour and the social problems of his time. He was able to reach a large number of people with his ideas because he made black and white prints of his paintings and sold them at much lower prices than the paintings themselves. His works can be seen in galleries in London, Liverpool, Birmingham, Edinburgh and other city galleries in Britain, and in the USA. Picture **26**, page 23.

Charles van Loo (1705–65) French
Van Loo came from a French family of artists who originally came from Belgium. He experimented with many different subjects in his paintings. His works can be seen in the Louvre, Paris, and in the National and Courtauld Institute Galleries in London. Picture **9**, page 10.

Edouard Manet (1832–83) French
Manet was a painter who greatly influenced the younger artists of his day. He himself had been influenced by earlier Spanish artists, especially their way of using light and dark colours. His works can be seen in major collections all over the world, especially the Louvre and Musée d'Orsay in Paris and the National and Courtauld Institute Galleries, London. Pic. **27**, p. 24.

Claude Monet (1840–1926) French
The leading Impressionist painter. His painting *Impression: Sunrise*, which was first shown in 1874, gave the name to the Impressionist movement. Monet's works can be seen in galleries throughout the world, and especially in Musées Marmottan and d'Orsay in Paris, France. Cover picture.

Rembrandt van Rijn (1606–69) Dutch
One of the greatest of all Dutch painters. One of his most famous paintings is the *Night Watch*, a huge group portrait of Amsterdam citizens. Throughout his career he painted portraits of himself which accurately reflected his advancing years and changed mood. His work can be seen in galleries all over the world, especially in the Netherlands, at the National Gallery and Wallace Collection in London, and in Cambridge, Edinburgh, Glasgow, Liverpool and Dublin. Picture **25**, page 23.

Jan Vermeer (1632–1675) Dutch
Until about the 1900s Vermeer's works were almost completely forgotten, but he is now considered to be one of the world's greatest painters. His works can be seen in major art collections around the world, including the Rijksmuseum and Mauritshuis in the Netherlands, and in the National Gallery and Kenwood House in London. Picture **24**, page 22.

Andy Warhol (c1928–1987) American
An American artist associated with 'Pop Art', so-called because it used popular images and objects that people see and use every day. Warhol especially made use of familiar products such as tinned soup and newspaper photographs, often making bright coloured screen prints of them. His work can be seen in major collections of modern art. Picture **31**, page 27.

Glossary

Aboriginal Relating to the native Australian people.

Absinthe A strong alcoholic drink which used to be drunk in France because it was cheap. It has now been forbidden because of its poisonous effects.

Amerindians The various peoples already living in the Americas before the arrival of the Europeans in the 1500s.

Ancestors People in a family who are no longer alive, such as great-grandparents and their parents and grandparents.

Banquet A large, grand meal, usually for many people, often held to celebrate a special occasion.

Camera obscura A machine which takes in the light from a scene to make a picture of it on a screen inside a dark box, or on a wall in a dark room.

Carcass The dead body of an animal that has been slaughtered (killed) for food.

Christianity The religion which is based on the teachings of Jesus Christ. Followers of Christianity are called Christians.

Christmas The time when Christians remember the birth of Jesus Christ in AD 1. Christians celebrate by sharing meals together and giving presents.

Civilizations Stages in the development of the way people live together in groups.

Id al-Fitr The Muslim festival held every year to celebrate the end of Ramadan, the time of fasting, when Muslims eat no food during daylight hours.

Impressionists A group of artists painting at the end of the nineteenth century in France. They recorded their impressions of light and colour in their work.

Middle Ages The period between the end of the Roman Empire and the Renaissance, from about AD 500 to AD 1500.

Mount Vesuvius A volcano in Italy which, when it erupted in AD 79, destroyed the Roman cities of Pompeii and Herculaneum.

Oil Paint A type of paint in which the colour is held together with linseed or poppy seed oil.

Outline A line which is drawn around the whole outside of a shape.

Pop Art A type of art in the 1960s, in America and Europe, which took ideas and images from popular objects such as comics, advertisements and films.

Post-Impressionists Artists who came after the Impressionists and who were very much influenced by them. They tried to develop new ways of using colours and shapes.

Realistic Having a believable appearance.

Relief A picture which is raised or partly three-dimensional.

Renaissance A time of rediscovery in Europe of the ideas of Ancient Greece and Rome.

Roman Empire The territories ruled by Ancient Rome. The head of the Empire was called the emperor.

St Peter One of the apostles or special followers of Jesus Christ.

Screen print A print made by squeezing ink through fabric stretched over a screen where the pattern is masked by a stencil.

Still life A painting or drawing of still objects such as fruit, flowers etc.

Texture The appearance, in art, of how the surface of an object looks and feels.

Trompe l'oeil A French phrase meaning a picture which tricks the eye into believing it can see something which is not real.

Tropical A very hot climate, occurring in countries near the Equator.

Wood-block print A print made by cutting away areas of a block of wood to form a picture. When the block is covered with ink and pressed on to paper, the cut design is printed.

Books to read

The Book of Art – A Way of Seeing (Ernest Benn, 1979).

Every Picture Tells a Story by Rolf Harris (Phaidon, 1989).

Food – through the eyes of artists by Wendy and Jack Richardson (Macmillan, 1991).

Great Painters by Piero Ventura (Kingfisher, 1989).

Just Look . . . A Book about Paintings by Robert Cumming (Viking Kestrel, 1986).

Painting and Sculpture by Jillian Powell (Wayland, 1989).

Penguin Dictionary of Art and Artists by Peter and Linda Murray (Penguin, 1989).

20th Century Art by Jillian Powell (Wayland, 1989).

Index

Picture acknowledgements

The publishers have attempted to contact all copyright holders of the illustrations in this title, and apologise if there have been any oversights.

The photographs in this book were supplied by: Bridgeman Art Library cover, 4, 5, 9, 10, 11, 19, 20, 21, 22, 23(top), 24, 25, 27(both); Michael Holford © 6(top), 7, 15(lower); Ronald Sheridan Ancient Art and Architecture Library 8(both), 16(both), 17; Tate Gallery 23(lower); Wayland Picture Library 26; Werner Forman Archive 6(lower), 12, 13(both), 14, 15(top), 18. *Campbell's Soup* by Andy Warhol on page 27 appears by permission of the copyright holders © 1992 The Andy Warhol Foundation for the Visual Arts/ARS, New York.